Echoes

Aqkay

Published By Galaxy Books
Copyright © 2016 Aqkay
All rights reserved.
ISBN-13978-0-9935428-5-5
ISBN-10 0-9935428-5-9

Contents

God and I

When here was nothing
There was a God
Would there be nothing
There would be a God

Being Me has alas
Totally ruined me
Had I just not been
Imagine what would I be?

*

Alone

Summer winter spring times
Thunder lightning and rain
All the human feelings
Happiness, sorrow and pain

Immeasurable universe
A code, none can parse
Are all these realities?
or simply just a farce

Dazzling bright sunshine
Full moon and the stars
Cities filled with noises
People buildings and cars

Moving like a shadow
In the morning mist
I often wish to know
Do I really exist?

Standing by the roadside,
I watch the traffic go by
Smiling to hide the pain
an effort not to cry

What if I am alone?
I am not the one who crawls
Whenever I want, I can
talk to my four walls

When I get up in the morning
I wonder more and more
Is it a new day or
have I lived it before?

Every thing I create
is merely an illusion
I ask my own questions
I make the conclusion

I create my friends, my foes
My sister and my brother
My happiness, my sorrows
Without a bit of a bother

I make the rules for myself
What's right and what is wrong
For me everything is real
My conviction is so strong

*

11th of September

11th of September
The day we remember
When sanity was on target
Who can ever forget?
How a dying child cried
The day the innocence died

Helpless people waving
Fire every where raging
Can one be so cruel?
Such a crazy fool
Who else could have tried?
The day the innocence died

Every eye filled with tear
Faces drawn, white with fear
Dust, smoke and rubble
Anger, pain and trouble
In fire, was humanity fried
The day the innocence died

*

My long lost friend

On a railway station
Bustling with activities
passengers, trains
noise and chaos
I stood helpless
Like a newly hatched
motherless chicken

Trying to feel
my way through
I saw you
A lonely girl
dressed in blue
with blue eyes
hair like gold
Our eyes met
We needed no introduction
We were long lost friends
who had never met before

We boarded the train
and started to talk
or rightly said
you started to talk
I just watched you
talking eagerly
like an innocent little girl
A wild stream
flowing noisily
down the hill

Suddenly your station arrived
You smiled and
disembarked silently
Train started to move
I saw you over again

A lonely girl in blue
Walking like an angel
My long lost friend
I'll never lose you

*

Spring

Rain,
flooding down bucket-full
Fierce wind
howling and scrubbing
the swaying trees
like a mother humming
while bathing her
naughty babies.

The Sun
wakes up
from its deep slumber
and peeps down
through the blanket
of dark clouds
to see
what the commotion was about.

Snowdrops
jump out eagerly
to greet the
first ray of sunshine

Crocus
follows suite
and starts to glitter
like colorful gems
in the sunlight.

It looks
so beautiful that
the Sun forgets its sleep
and rolls away
the dirty blanket of clouds
The sky becomes clear blue
and the Sun starts to shine

Daffodils
start the invasion
and cover every nook and crook
of the gray wintry land
with their beautiful golden flowers.

Tulips
shoot up hurriedly
not to miss the show
and come into flower
in all the possible colors

Cherry,
plum and apple trees
Blossom up
in a rush
and stand in awe
like big flower bouquets
to hail the Sun

Trees,
sheepishly
start to show
their buds
And leaves
start to sprout
A green rug of grass
Is soon spread
on the ground

Migratory birds
receive the good news
that the spring is in the air
They speedily arrive

Linnet and the Goldfinch
lead and Dunnock, Blackbird,
Greenfinch Blue Tit and the Coal Tit
Join in to sing in their
melodious spring concert

Rose,
the queen of flowers,
followed by,
Poppy, Agapanthus,
Amaryllis, Anemone, Bird of Paradise,
Calla lily, Corn flower, Dahlia, Delphinium,
Pussy willow and Seeded Eucalyptus
enter the stage
to sing the glory
of the spring
that has sprung.

*

Come back

My cat my little teddy bear
Always ask me Papa dear
Dad, why you had to go?
Oh, I constantly miss you so
Its summer here and full moon
Papa please, come back soon

I will not go to bed late
I will not eat any chocolate
I promise, I will not cry
If my sister eats my pie
Not even for a balloon
Papa please, come back soon

I dream of you every night
Just come, everything will be right
We used to go to the zoo
Singing aloud song, just we two
I want to hear that charming tune
Papa please, come back soon

If you don't come, I will be sad
I will not talk to you, Dad
Even if you may try and try
I will sit alone and cry
Every day from morning till noon
Papa please, come back soon

*

Nature

Summer turns into autumn
Winter brings the spring
Cold nights are forgotten
Birds begin to sing
Blue sky, sun, rolling hills
Flowers, all over you see
Nature is in everything
Around you and me

Peaceful moonlit nights
Blanket of stars above
No sound to hear except
A lovely song of dove
Soothing every soul
Filling up with glee
Nature is in everything
Around you and me

Earthquakes and tornados
Attacks of locust swarms
Floods, famine and diseases
Droughts, lightning and storms
Remind us of its might
How monstrous it can be
Nature is in everything
Around you and me

*

Tipsy

Lovers often lie
They can cheat
It is true
They do it because
they are afraid
to say adieu

Tears cannot
drown all sorrows
They don't do
Why keep them
falling like an
early morning dew

Wine intoxicates
Life? It does too
Someone drinks
I am alive
We are high
Yes, we two

*

Now

Enjoy every day
every night
every hour
every second
of this precious gift
your life

Don't sit and
wait for a better
time to come
It is now
this moment
the best time
you have it
grab it

If you don't enjoy
the night
will be soon over
It will become
Just a tale
not a soul will
bother to listen
it will become so stale

*

Lark

Cheerful, as I am always
Flying through the cloud
Sailing with the wind
Singing my song aloud

Worries don't bother me
Sorrow have I none
Why should I be sorry?
When I have the sun

I enjoy being optimist
See bright things in the dark
It keeps me so happy
They call me a lark

*

Smile

Economic down turn
disease famine and war
Bad news at the doorstep
you don't have to go far
Face the depressing world
with a brand new style
Just take a deep breath
and smile a big smile

We spend our evenings
watching TV alone
Instead of visiting friends
we talk on the phone
Why do we turn into a
lonely isolated isle
Just take a deep breath
and smile a big smile

Whenever you are fallen
all the odds are down
Don't sit and shed tears
never ever do frown
Bravely face injustice
Everything that's hostile
Just take a deep breath
and smile a big smile

In the race for money
greed, lust and pleasure
Everyone wants to be
a man of a stature
What are we actually doing?
Please think for a while
Just take a deep breath
and smile a big smile

Our world is blessed with
a breathtaking beauty
To keep this one cheerful
it is our foremost duty
Let us make it worth living
it doesn't have to be vile
Just take a deep breath
and smile a big smile

*

Future

Everybody is talking
Talking about the future
They just talk, talk
and simply go away

What is the future?
A wise man's vision
A poet's wild dream
A shadow of yesterday

Past has surely gone
Present is still here
Let's shape it into a future
Far better than today

*

Not for sale

You force women to sell their bodies
Enslave laborers by the lure of wage
You can buy everything in the world
Have you money for this single page?

Can you repay a mother for her love?
Breathe life into a plastic doll?
Just tell me what you can give for
all the colors in the fall?

I gave wings to my thoughts
Told them secret of my existence
Gave them my flesh and my blood
From the flowers, I took fragrance

Blushes from an innocent face
free flight from a little feather
colors from the beautiful rainbow
and mixed all of them together

Like a symphony by thousand violins
My own novel poetry was born
You say you can pay for my verses
For this foolishness you should mourn

*

Why

This world is a stage
Everyone here is an actor
Some are good some bad
Many of them are real mad
But the victors do never try
Can someone tell me why?

Everybody is worried
We are eating too much
Our children are crazy about
Coke, junk food and such
Hungry children in Africa
are left alone to die
Can someone tell me why?

It's an era of freedom
Full of words yet unspoken
Where are those white doves?
Their pretty wings are broken
They will never fly
Can someone tell me why?

*

Desire

Why is everyone's life
so chockfull of desire?
We're burned to ashes
by this eternal fire

From every dawn to dust
we slave for the vampire
Our bodies are prisons
ringed by this barbed wire

Our visions, our thoughts
are focused to acquire
we have no time for
natures stunning attire

Nobody tells us alas
to relax and just admire
Let love be our guide
Nature lead our choir

*

Dandelion

Trampled and forsaken
I watch people goby
No one glances at me
As much as I may try

I have many acquaintances
But I have no real friend
Whenever I seek someone
I'm shunned in the end

I long for care and love
But none will ever know
This is my sad secret
My head will never bow

I can't sleep whole night
My heart is full of pain
But I am a Dandelion
I will rise up again

*

Let's dance

Come and dance my love
We are young and night long
Spring is in the air and
they are playing our song

Look the stars are shining
like diamonds in the sky
My lonely heart is   begging
say you love me, don't deny

Life is long but full of
miseries, sorrows and fear
It's our precious moment
grab it and enjoy my dear

Time is fleeting it never
Stops, even for a while
So why don't we enjoy it,
have a nice time and smile

*

Happiness

O happiness! How we
always long for you
But what you really are
None of us has a clue

We know that we were happy
exactly when in the past
But when we are happy
time always passes so fast

We always feel that others
are happier than we are
We try to get you even
we have to wage war

We seek you every where
In wealth, fame and pride
But few of us ever know
Real happiness lives inside

*

A dream

I dreamt of you
again last night
You were you and
I was I myself
last night

Spring was in the air
flowers every where
We were
very young and stupid
last night

Laughing like
we used to do
we were
really happy
last night

We danced
in the moonlight
Swaying in
each other's arms
last night

You were telling me
You loved me
And all other
such lies
last night

I was so glad
to hear your tales
I didn't care
Whether they
were false
last night

I dreamt of you
last night
I dreamt of us
last night

Echoes

*

My past

Time is fleeting by
It never stops
Not even to
let me have a
glimpse of my past

Past that was
so full of fear,
pain, anxiety
and an endless
longing for you

I used to wish
earnestly that I
someday somehow
would forget
my dreadful past

But now,
when time is erasing it
from my memory
I am not letting it
do the work

Like a drowning man
I am trying
to catch this
last straw…
My past

*

Diva

Standing in front of a mirror
She eagerly sings a song
In an imaginary concert
which will be whole night long

She is nine but sings like
a pop star in her prime
She opens her tiny mouth
and the bells start to chime

She may lack a bit in rhythm,
pitch may not be so right
But she covers it up with
passion and a will to fight

She bows to an imaginary,
large and cheering crowd
Finally ends her concert
contented, happy and proud

She sings every day for
sisters, mama and papa
everyone is so sure that
she is a little diva

*

My jewels

My woes are
my jewels,
glittering and fine
I am happy to
wear them
with pride

Why should I
hide my tears,
They are meant
for running,
They will run
They should run

Complain?
I never do
If I want to be alive
I'll have to
bear the brunt
and suffer

My melancholies
Are so happy to
be with me
I often wonder,
where will they go
when I am gone?
Who will be
happy to wear
my precious jewels?

*

Leave me alone

Among so many
good people
I am the only one
who is bad

Everyone can
sing beautifully
I am the one
who cannot
carry a tune

I once tried to
glance inside myself
I cannot describe
how horrifying
experience it was

Yes,
you all are
virtuous and truthful
I am the only one
who is a liar

Go away
and worship
the statues of
your own
greatness

Please
leave me alone
I am so bad
So bad
And you are
so good
So good

*

Without you

Whenever you go away
You take my peace with you
My sleep is gone, I lay
awake, as lovers do

My life is meaningless,
joyless misery and toil
I have no clue how to
cope up with this turmoil

I wander on the beach
in the moonlit night
Like a headless chicken
In the shimmering moonlight

 I try to imagine you're
with me, but I feel pain
How can one cheat oneself?
My efforts are in vain

They say I must forget
But I don't know how-to
None can take your place
Nothing compares to you

*

My love

I searched
heaven and earth
but couldn't find
my one and only
sweetheart

Does she
really exist
or It is just a
wild creation of
my fantasy?

Her image
is always
In my mind
I can see her
clearly like a
high definition picture
on the TV screen

I think
I have seen her
several times
Where?
I don't remember
In my dreams
or in reality?
I am not sure

But one thing
I surely know
She is mine
and she will
always remain
my one and only love

*

Name

In a little far off village
Lives a very pretty dame
She is my one and only love
But I have forgotten her name

I try always to talk to her
But she sadly pays no heed
Why it is so I don't know
It's a complex mystery indeed

All my friends tease me endlessly
day and night, to their hearts fill
Just wait my friends, I say to them
She'll be mine one day, she will

But nights are long, I yearn for her
my heart aches and I cannot sleep
I lie awake and wonder how
to forget her love and not weep

One fine and sunny morning when I
was rambling along the lonely street
I saw her walking with her friends
I ran forward joyfully to greet

Lo and behold, I remembered
her name, Lisa ! I gladly screamed
She came to me and we hugged
I have her now as I'd dreamed

*

The Wind

Blow, blow, blow,
this freezing day, O wind!
I wish that she wouldn't be
with poor me so chagrined

This world be so forlorn
If she wouldn't be my girl
O Lord she is so sweet
A gem, a diamond a pearl

I try to be as kind
as a young lad could be
Oh look what luck I have
She also smiles at me

I asked her last evening
Will you dear, marry me?
She smiled and saw yes love
Your glad wife I will be

Blow, blow, blow,
on wedding day, O wind!
I am glad she wouldn't be
with lucky me so chagrined

*

Transformation

When every thing is going
right as I had planned
I feel I am a god
Supreme, almighty and grand

Every one praises me
admirations know no bound
All I touch becomes gold
I tread on holy ground

Suddenly out of nowhere
comes a calamity profound
it shatters me like twigs
spread on a mound

No one praises me now
Their admiration is gone
They've found another god
I am no longer their Khan

What a transformation
From a god to a scum bag,
a worm, a rat, a skunk
Eluded like a filthy rag

I sit and wonder a lot
What on earth have I done?
Who controls my destiny?
Surely, I am not the one

*

Clown

Happy as a lark
Flying through the cloud
Sailing with the wind
Cheerily singing aloud

I think of you and I am
The loneliest man in town
Why did you build me up?
Just to tear me down

When I try to sleep
My eyes don't even close
Your vision comes to me
like a fresh red rose

I try to forget you but
recall a bridal gown
Why did you build me up?
Just to tear me down

Friends try to console me
They say I will retrieve
How can they say this?
Why are they so naive?

No one laughs at me
But I feel like a clown
Why did you build me up?
Just to tear me down

*

Secrets

Paper kite, teddy bear,
red car, cycle and jeep
They always keep watch
When I go to sleep
People say they don't thrive
I know...They all are alive

My papa is strongest
person on the earth
He is awfully wise and
Brainy from his birth
He can add two and two
There's nothing... he can't do

When I will grow up
I will become like him
I will travel a lot
Every sea I will swim
One thing I wouldn't do
That, I will not tell you

*

Children of the rainbow

(A Norwegian Song)

A sky full of stars,
blue sea as far as you can see
An earth where flowers grow,
can you wish for more?
Together shall we live,
every sister, brother, you and me
Young children of the rainbow,
a fertile land and seashore

Some believe it is useless,
others waste time just talking
Some think we can live on
plastics and synthetic food
Some steal from the youngsters,
who are sent out for fighting
Several steal from the many,
which are still backward and crude

A sky full of stars,
blue sea as far as you can see
An earth where flowers grow,
can you wish for more?
Together shall we live,
every sister, brother, you and me
Young children of the rainbow,
a fertile land and seashore

But tell all the kids,
and say it to fathers and mother every
To share peace and the earth,
this is our last opportunity

A sky full of stars,
blue sea as far as you can see
An earth where flowers grow,
Can you wish for more?

*

Wake up

Wake up my dear people wake up
Get up and give a good fight
They are putting us in boxes,
Blacks in black and whites in white

Oh, why do not they understand?
We all are precisely the same
We have similar behaviors and feelings
Happiness, anger, pride and shame
They always want to submit us
To a never ending plight

Wake up my dear people wake up,
Get up and give a good fight
They are putting us in boxes,
Blacks in black and whites in white

They first attempt to divide us
Then they try their best to rule
By injecting in our hearts, hatred
an abundantly available fuel
Unluckily we can never spot it
But it at all times does ignite

Wake up my dear people wake up,
Get up and give a good fight
They are putting us in boxes,
Blacks in black and whites in white

This world will be so cool, so cool
When we will live in harmony
There will be peace everywhere on earth
We shall live in an eternal glory
Shout loud my people shout loud
This is your straightforward birthright

Wake up my dear people wake up,
Get up and give a good fight
They are putting us in boxes,
Blacks in black and whites in white

Wake up my dear people wake up,
Get up and give a good fight
They are putting us in boxes,
Blacks in black and whites in white

*

Sweet home

An empty house
Bare and forsaken
Melancholic and lifeless
Reminiscent of an
ancient derelict
church cemetery

No chime of laughter
No sigh,
No moan
No clang of the shattering glass
Just an appalling silence
Intermittently broken by
the flutter of a curtain
rustling in the wind
from an open window

Marks of the
pictures on the wall
furniture on the carpet
dried petals from
the flowers and plants
My cherished possessions
Collected with care
love and affections
It was my sweet home
You changed it into a house
by closing the door behind you

When and why it happened
I have no word left to say
But in my sleepless nights
when you wander through
the deserted memory lane of mine
This lonely house transforms
back to my home, sweet home

*

Hush

Oh that lethal hush again
Why the birds stopped chirping?
No sound of thunder
No rumble down under
Just a ghastly... silence
Deadly and piercing

Where are the children?
Their toys, dolls and the clown
With their little mischief
Without any trace of grief
Naughty and cute faces
Where have they all gone?

Let there be some noise
I will hear joyous cries
Play loudly the drums,
flutes, violins and thrums
I don't want to listen to
my damned wailing, my sighs

*

Urban Tarzan

Clad in a tight black leather suit,
he jumps onto the bonnet
and then roof of the oncoming car
Jumping from car top to car top,
he crosses the road
filled with a multitude
of fast moving vehicles,
reminiscent of the noisy
angry bees flying out of a
beehive under attack

With a loud howl of ecstasy
he jumps onto the saddle
of his gleaming Harley Davidson
and darts like a shooting star
at a speed of 100 miles per hour
in the 30 miles per hour zone

The hunt is on
Urban Tarzan,
the king of the
metropolitan roads,
is ready for the kill
Beware! He is looking for
his prey, any prey.

*

Exploration

Last night I tried
to have a deep look
into myself
To make out
what is real Me?
Who lives inside there?
How does he feel?
What are his desires?
What gives him joy?
What causes him pain?
Why he likes some
and dislikes others?
To investigate
what he is really like
An expedition of mine
into myself.

It was a long
and tiresome journey
into a known unknown
Without any guide,
trail, map or compass
Just the shadow of doubt
to lead one astray into
an infinite abyss of time.

I met a stranger there
seemingly,
a very conceited and
confused personality
Who desires to be
higher than others,
even by standing on the
top of their corpses

Who is filled with joy
when he sees others
not as fortunate as
he thinks he is

Who likes
only those,
who say what
he wants to hear

Who, if he sees
the same faults in others,
as he has in himself,
hates them.

I often wonder
whether he
really is such

Or are these
just masks
he wears to hide
himself from this
harsh world?

Or simply
he mirrors
the true image
of us and
our society?

*

Memory lane

I by no means feel lost and lonely
walking down the memory lane
My thoughts circle over my head
like mosquitoes after the rain
My sorrows are there too
so are worries, my life's bane

I see faces, long lost, around me
shadows in the shimmering light
My friends, my foes all are there
with whom I used to play and fight
I wish to hold them, talk to them
but they drift away like a kite

My failures and successes are dancing together
strangely, they both look all the same
No success brings any more pleasure
for the failures, I don't feel any shame
I laugh when I remember all efforts
to find an excuse, to shift the blame

Suddenly I see a bright light
like a sunray through a dark cloud
I see you at the end of the lane
my love, drifting in the mob
Then I know my journey is over
I have met my heart throb

*

Light

I had a dream
This dream was not
dreamt during a
peaceful night's sleep
It was dreamt
during the broad day light
with open eyes

The light was so bright
and the shadows so dark
that the landscape seemed
like a black and white picture
All the colours were there
but they had become harsh
tormenting and meaningless
Everything was real
but seemed so surreal

I saw people moving
silently like shadows
Everybody looked scared
Scared to talk
Scared to have an eye contact
Scared to walk
Scared to show affection
Scared to acknowledge any smile
Scared to make a connection

Drifting here and there
Hidden
in their own shells
like sea turtles
wandering aimlessly
on a remote
and lonely island

Strangely they all
looked alike
Same age
Same look
Same height
Same figure
Same colour
Same clothes
Even the same voice
You see one
and you have
seen them all

Although they all
were totally strangers
yet they looked
so familiar
I decided to
go ahead
and meet them

First one I met
had his face
in the shadow
I turned his face
towards the light

I was amazed
at what I saw
Looking at his face
was like
gazing in the mirror

Same age
Same look
Same height
Same figure
Same colour
Same clothes
Even the same voice
He was an exact replica of mine

I glanced at the crowd again
I was astounded to see how
all of them had transformed

Everybody looked afraid
Afraid to talk
Afraid to have an eye contact
Afraid to acknowledge any smile
Afraid to make a connection
They all had become
Me or I had become them

The king is dead
Long live the king

*

Conversation

I often speak:

With friends,
to say a lot
but mean nothing.

With strangers,
believing it is with you.

With my dear mates,
to be hurt again.

With walls,
in my loneliness.

With flowers,
whenever I remember you.

I never utter any word.
The sound of silence
like the African drums
conveys my message
completely and unambiguously
far better than any spoken word

Everyone is contented.
I am delighted
because my idiocy
is not revealed
They are pleased
as they hear
what they want to hear

Echoes

*

Is it love

I like you
I miss you
I want to see you
I want to be with you
I am always
thinking about you
Is it love?

Every moment in a day
or in the dark of the lonely night
you are on my mind
You are the only one
who I think
is my real friend
Is it love?

Whenever you are
by my side
the beating of my heart
like a jungle drum
strives to convey
a message to you
Dum-de dumm dumm
I love you
Dum-de dumm dumm
I love you
Is it love?

*

Another summer

So, it is the end of
another summer
Bright sunny days
and long warm nights
are slowly becoming shorter
Sunlight, dimmer and dimmer
like the last flicker of
a burnt up candle

Trees are hastily
changing their attire
from shabby green to
all possible hues of
gold and red
in order to participate
in the fashion parade
every evening
just before the sunset

Most of the birds
have already flown
to the warmer places
Those left behind
are in such a hurry
to join them that
they have forgotten
their melodious songs

Morning mist has
started to invade
the shivering shadows
waiting in long queues
for the busses and trains
which are delayed
due to the reasons
known to none

The icy winds
of the long cold winter
will soon freeze up
the warm memories
of the sun
but deep in our heart somewhere
we will still have the
longing to go back
where it all had begun
The summer will
carry on forever
It will never be
forgotten

***